6	7	8	9	10
16	17	18	19	20
26	27	28	29	30
36	37	38	39	40
46	47	48	49	50
56	57	58	59	60
66	67	68	69	70
76	77	78	79	80
86	87	88	89	90
96	97	98	99	100

Library of Congress Cataloging-in-Publication Data:
Mathieu, Joseph.
Sesame Street 1 2 3 / Joe Mathieu.   p.   cm. SUMMARY: Characters from Sesame
Street appear in a variety of situations that provide the opportunity to count.
ISBN 0-679-81230-X (trade) — ISBN 0-679-91230-4 (lib. bdg.)
1. Counting—Juvenile literature. [1. Counting.] I. Children's Television Workshop.
II. Title III. Title: Sesame Street 1 2 3
QA113.M37 1991 513.5'5—dc20 [E] 91-1992

Manufactured in the United States of America   10 9 8 7 6 5 4 3 2

A Counting Book from 1 to 100

illustrated by Joe Mathieu

Random House/CTW

1 broom sweeping, swooshing

2 hammers pounding, pounding

3 big bales of hay

4 round rubber tires

5 fleas flitting, flying

6 wet works of art
Don't touch, please.

7 jars of finger paint

8 trash treasures for sale

9 slimy worms in a band

10 tops dripping, drying

12 bats flying around

13 cards lying facedown

14 clumps of clay

15 drying pots

16 rubber duckies

17 wind-up froggies

18 wonderful prizes

19 stuffed animals sitting pretty

20 softballs ready to toss

30 apples

40 apple tarts

50 bottles of Figgy Fizz

60 striped straws
Whoops!

LEMONS
LEMONS
LEMONS
LEMONS LEMONS
LEMONS LEMONS

Lemonade 10¢

80 flags for fluttering, flying

90 balloons

Where are they going?

To the Sesame Street Fair!

100 Twiddlebugs at the Twiddlebug Fair!

1	2	3	4	5
11	12	13	14	15
21	22	23	24	25
31	32	33	34	35
41	42	43	44	45
51	52	53	54	55
61	62	63	64	65
71	72	73	74	75
81	82	83	84	85
91	92	93	94	95